I DREAMED I WAS
EMILY DICKINSON'S BOYFRIEND

I DREAMED I WAS
EMILY DICKINSON'S BOYFRIEND

Poems

Ron Koertge

Red Hen Press | *Pasadena, CA*

Layout by Isiah Lyons

Library of Congress Cataloging-in-Publication Data

Names: Koertge, Ronald, author.
Title: I dreamed I was Emily Dickinson's boyfriend: poems / Ron Koertge.
Description: First edition. | Pasadena, CA: Red Hen Press, [2022]
Identifiers: LCCN 2022007283 (print) | LCCN 2022007284 (ebook) | ISBN
    9781636280332 (hardcover) | ISBN 9781636280905 (paperback) | ISBN
    9781636280349 (ebook)
Subjects: LCGFT: Poetry.
Classification: LCC PS3561.O347 I3 2022 (print) | LCC PS3561.O347 (ebook)
    | DDC 811/.54—dc23/eng/20220211
LC record available at https://lccn.loc.gov/2022007283
LC ebook record available at https://lccn.loc.gov/2022007284

The National Endowment for the Arts, the Los Angeles County Arts Commission, the Ahmanson Foundation, the Dwight Stuart Youth Fund, the Max Factor Family Foundation, the Pasadena Tournament of Roses Foundation, the Pasadena Arts & Culture Commission and the City of Pasadena Cultural Affairs Division, the City of Los Angeles Department of Cultural Affairs, the Audrey & Sydney Irmas Charitable Foundation, the Meta & George Rosenberg Foundation, the Albert and Elaine Borchard Foundation, the Adams Family Foundation, Amazon Literary Partnership, the Sam Francis Foundation, and the Mara W. Breech Foundation partially support Red Hen Press.

    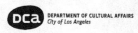

First Edition
Published by Red Hen Press
www.redhen.org

Acknowledgments

3rd Wednesday: "Mannequin"; *Bridge Eight*: "All the News," "I Like to Kiss," "Red Riding Hood's Mother"; *Columbia Review*: "Jane Austen at the Mall," "Piece Work from the Garment Factory"; *Congeries*: "Judging the Student Film Festival," "Men at Work," "Last Night"; *Court Green*: "I Dreamed I Was Emily Dickinson's Boyfriend," "My Friends and I Wanted to Be Movie Stars," "The Cat Who Doesn't Like Anybody But My Wife Lolls in Ezra Pound's Lap," "The Wasp Woman"; *Fourteen Hills*: "After the Funeral"; *I-70 Review*: "Double Vision"; *Interlitq*: "from *The Secret Diaries of Mary Wollstonecraft Shelley*"; *Lummox*: "Secrets My Students Have Told Me"; *Nerve Cowboy*: "Can You Tell Us a Little About Your Wife?"; and *Rattle*: "Things and How They Work."

Thanks to Kim, Charles, and Jan for their keen eyes.

Thanks to Bianca for everything

Contents

I

II

III

IV

I

I Dreamed I Was Emily Dickinson's Boyfriend

Our love is secret, so we go to the movies all the way over
in Greenfield, then stop by the Fun Zone.

Emily kills at foosball. That gossamer and tulle makes
guys think she can't play.

We talk at least once a day. When I ask her what she did
she says, "Stayed indoors."

The other night she texted me, "I feel a funeral in my brain.
But come over, anyway, and we'll watch ESPN."

She tells me I'm more fun than Reverend Charles Wadsworth,
and a better kisser than Judge Lord.

She asks for help with her poetry. Hope is a thing with . . .
1. Fur 2. Down 3. Feathers 4. An exoskeleton

She's older than me so she can buy beer at any 7-Eleven. She likes
a liquor never brewed. Which 7-Eleven doesn't carry.

She gives me little books of her poems that she's sewn
together herself.

"Keep these, honey," she says. "They'll be worth a lot
someday."

Parkview1- 9426

Remember when there was a pad of paper by the phone
and that was attached to the wall by a leash?

Usually there was a partial shopping list there or the date
of a doctor's appointment.

Sometimes the small pages were torn away, but when they
weren't they made up a short

illustrated diary featuring the ever-popular stars and bolts
of lightning. Snowmen never went out of style

or stick figures holding hands. Of course heading the list
of doodles should be initials

inside of lopsided hearts, usually with one of Cupid's
darts piercing the left atrium

but every now and then the darts turned to arrows, many
arrows with wicked-looking barbs

to show how wrong love can go while simply talking
on the telephone.

The Wasp Woman

Janice Starlin, owner of a foundering cosmetics firm,
is injected with royal jelly from wasps. She grows younger
until the headaches start. Then she needs more, so much
that she turns into a carnivorous insect and devours
the nearest man.

She's killed, of course, and the status quo is restored.
Bill and Mary from Accounting continue dating
but the relationship doesn't go anywhere. He saved her
life, yes, but now he lies around the apartment in a T-shirt
with a stain on it.

Maureen from the typing pool has to find work elsewhere.
From a distance she almost looks like a movie star. She's hired
quickly but calls in sick a lot. She has nightmares and is fired.

It's that way with everyone who worked at Starlin Enterprises,
everyone who even glimpsed the wasp woman. The account
executive cries in the market buying his frozen dinner.

The kid who brought in bagels turns to a life of petty crime.
The fat janitor was first to be eaten. All the police found
was his hat which they gave to his wife.

No pension from the company. Just a hat. And what
is she supposed to do with that as the bills pour in
and the buzzing in her ears gets louder and louder?

Death's Hankies

Imagine how many of them he goes
through in a day.

Good ones, bleached cotton, soft,
easy on the eyes, easy on the nose.

Dozens in his dark car. Used ones
in a spotless laundry bag.

Every night the washer churns
and unless it's raining he hangs

them out behind his blue house
on a line that sags just a little.

Mermaids

Mitch and I worked the ice cream stand at the pool that summer
and when he saw me checking out two girls in impossible bikinis
he said, "Forget it, man. They're way out of our league."

When we closed up, there they were asking for a ride.
They were still wet and they smelled good.

We were flying down that hill by the lake when one said,
"See if you can scare us."

Mitch gunned his old Camaro onto the grass between
the picnic tables and toward the long dock. They're screaming
like girls who are having fun but that changed when we went
right off the end.

Water poured in. We fought with our seat belts. The one with me
yelled, "Abby, remember that movie we saw in Rome? Wait till
the car fills up and we can probably swim out."

Instead of drowning, I thought about Rome. Coliseums, Catholics,
pizza. I sat as still as I could as the water rose and rose.

"*Buono*," she said. "Hold your breath now." So I did and before
the car rolled onto its side we slithered through the windows.

Mitch and I clawing our way up. Abby and the other one holding
hands like mermaids, things at home in another world entirely.

Girl Talk

My mother tells me to be careful about who I hang out with and what I do because "it can all come back and bite you in the ass." My friends think my mother is "earthy" and "hilarious" and also "poisonous." Anyway, I'm getting advice from somebody who has been married three times and cries herself to sleep. She makes me never want to have a kid and if somebody just handed me a baby and then hopped into a red convertible with a license plate that said SUPERFUN, I'd go right to the nearest fire station and drop the kid off. But I'd go alone because my mom loves firemen and watches every show on TV that has sirens. If she went along with me to the fire station, the next morning I'd be eating oatmeal and a stranger in a very red helmet would stroll in and sheepishly introduce himself. The other day in the computer lab, I looked up animals that mate for life instead of three-day weekends in Palm Springs. Here's what I found: Black vultures, French angelfish, Gibbons, Swans, Wolves, Termites, Beavers, Prairie Voles, Bald eagles, Barn owls. I imagined everything on that list getting together at a Holiday Inn and celebrating their devotedness. They're all so different there wouldn't be any jealousy though I can imagine the wolves might want to eat the voles but since the wolf-husband has been married a long time he would know you can't just do what you want so he'd wait till the buffet was available so as not to ruin the weekend for everybody, even the termites. The other day Mom asked me if I knew about condoms and as a joke I said, "Sure. The best ones taste like strawberry." And she said, "Oh, my God, honey. Me too." Then she hugged me. And I couldn't help it. I hugged her back.

Lover's Lane

It was a place we'd heard about from older
boys, so Rusty and I rode our bikes through
town, then down the hill that was so treacherous
in winter.

We wound through some trees and one hundred yards
of muddy ruts: beer bottles, a picnic table
carved up by romantic vandals: names, hearts,
swastikas.

"Stupid," Rusty said. "Probably different at night,"
I told him. He said, "Maybe."

It wasn't that bad: lots of birds, quiet not yet
roughed up by the day.

When we heard a car, we hid. An Oldsmobile
moving so slow it might have been a big animal
grazing.

I whispered, "Holy crap, that's your dad!"

We turned our backs on them, crept deeper
into the woods and pretended to read some comics
I'd brought.

Superman saving the world again, Lois
in his arms, forsaking all others and holding
only onto him.

When my wife's brother Richard passed, he left our son a train set. We opened the many boxes full of tracks and roads. Factories and houses. Little figures who lived in an elaborate community. Our son was enthralled as we put everything together. Richard included various hats that he wore when he was presiding over his train set. An engineer's cap, of course. And a blue policeman's hat with a small, shiny bill. That's the one our son wore constantly. "School zone," he'd say as I hurried through the living room. Or, if his mother was sitting down to watch her favorite TV show called *Sarcastic Judge*, he'd say, "No loitering, Let's see some ID." My wife and I lay awake whispering about what a little Nazi he'd become. At dinner he'd written me up for taking a baked potato hostage. So one evening after the news I found him in the basement where the train set took up every inch of space. I said, "Don't you think you're taking this law enforcement thing a little too seriously?" He sighed, sounding like a much older, much heavier man. He pointed at the cracked mirror that stood in for a pond. "We found little Becky Turrell's body this morning. Where were you on the night of the twenty-sixth?"

The Search Party

It's hopeless. Maureen and I broke up
again. While the party goes on
without me, I'm sulking in the kitchen

eating all the chips and guacamole
when the host's daughter comes in.

Nora opens the door to the refrigerator.
There's a stuffed bear leaning on the cottage
cheese.

She says, "That's Robert Falcon Scott,
the explorer. He needs medical attention
ASAP."

She looks at me. "Can I trust you to wait
right here while I go for the huskies?"

Now I cannot leave my post. Not to dance,
not to make a beer run. Not even if someone
says she likes my new shirt.

Nora returns with two stuffed dogs. The door
to Antarctica opens.

Nora cradles the bear. She tries to feed it
a Cheeto. "Hold on, Robert. Help
is on the way."

To me, she says, "Harness the dogs.
We have to move fast."

It's starting to snow. My hands are freezing
as I untangle the tow lines.

Bears from Space

Plastic honey bears on every table in every coffee shop. Nanoparticles in the yellow nozzles send information back to Constellation Ursa. Thousands of bears are on alert. Our space ships stand ready. When the bear-ships land—huge, monolithic, imposing—humans will go to their knees. They will roll over and show their fat, white stomachs. Only one thing from coffee shop data is worrisome: most hominids tip the little bear and squeeze. But a few rip the bear's hat off and dip a spoon into its skull. This suggests a savagery that must be taken into account. Perhaps they are not as naked and puny as they appear.

Mannequin

Anyone can do anything they want with me. Caress me here and there. Carry me under their sweaty arms past the security guard who likes to feel me up. My job on this side of the big plate glass window is to inspire yearning. Women want to look like me—endlessly, effortlessly thin with a hundred outfits. I am the most seductive in the rain. Safe and warm with somebody to dress me. Speaking of Luis and Teddy, they talk as they work. A disappointing movie, a mother ill in Minneapolis, gold in an underground river, the myth of love. Behind the scenes, stock boys like me in nothing but a fox fur hat, head tilted like I'm just asking to be slapped around. In the show window, I am chic though my arms are often at odd angles like I am trying to deflect a meteorite.

Noir ABCs

Asked the wrong guy
Blood on the library steps
Cops raid Jade Dragon Spa
Damsel in dis dress
Everybody locks eyes
For Christ's sake, rookie
Grieving tips from a pro
Hair, fingerprints, bodily fluids
It's a puzzler
Jokes turning to ash
Killer Snapchats satisfied sigh
Lilac bra shrine
Mantis-sex for a price
Nasty piece of work
Oh, no. Please. Wait
Party bus in shambles
Queen B abdicates
Run, you stinking coward
Sun taken away in cuffs
This isn't over yet, pal
Uber driver unmasked
Velma, just give me the gun
Wallet with holy cards
Xenophobe mixer at 10:00
Yearning is no excuse
Zip those pretty lips

Dear Mr. K

The reason I am writing is I keep seeing deeper meanings in your poems, but my friends say there's nothing there. In that one poem where you go to the race track, I think the rain stands for something but everybody says it's just rain. You can settle things if you are kind and want to write back. I saw your picture somewhere online and you look kind for an older old person. Do you do anything special to look not as old as you might look if you didn't do anything? Like a vitamin, maybe? I showed my father your poems. He said, "What?" See, that's an example of something my teacher calls compression: meaning a lot without saying a lot. Your poems are not very compressed. They are all over the place. They sprawl on the page like lazy cats. Do you like that simile? I sort of learned that from you. Okay, I agree with my father and nobody makes similes for a living. Or maybe I'm wrong. How much do you make per year. Or even per month. Or even per simile. If that's too nosy, pretend I didn't ask. I like you as a poet. You're very simple to read compared to famous poets. I showed my mother your poems, too. She laughed but not at the funny ones. Write back, okay? Soon if you can. My grandfather looked pretty good like you do but he died in church sitting up. Well, that's all for now. It's raining outside. If I was a poet it would probably stand for something but I'm not so it's just rain. Thank you.

Mickey

His shoes are always yellow and because he cavorts a lot
they wear out.

Saturday. His day off. He orders grilled cheese at a sidewalk café.
Watches the little tree at the curb breathing exhaust but still doing
its best. Leaves a big tip then goes shopping.

A salesman at Preposterous Kicks reports that Victor is in the hospital.
The new guy brings Mickey the wrong size. Tries to sell him wing tips.

Mickey decides to go by Cedars-Sinai. It's not visiting hours,
but the receptionist waves him through. The gift shop has a thousand
stuffed animals that recognize him.

Since he's a mouse with an excellent sniffer, he finds the right
room in a jiffy.

Mickey has never seen Victor lying down. And then there's Victor's
wife clutching a wad of tissues. Talk about awkward!

Mickey retreats. Tries to gambol away but his feet are leaden.
All he and Minnie do is hold hands. Or bang their noses together
in the semblance of a big smackeroo.

He pictures himself in a hospital: Minnie arranging flowers,
flirting with Dr. Goofy, or flipping through a fashion magazine.

He can't imagine her perky bow drooping, much less those enormous
eyes filled with tears.

After the Funeral

My sister and I stay to put the house
on the market.

Every night she dreams that a wolf comes
in and circles the Christmas tree three times.

The wolf is hungry and wants a dish of milk.
She wakes up and hurries to the kitchen.

In the morning, the milk is gone.

My sister decides to watch. She dozes
in the living room with a book.

In the morning, the milk is gone.

"It's like a fairy tale," she tells me.
"I can't keep my eyes open."

We decide to try together. The only light
comes from the tree's old-fashioned bulbs,
green and red mostly, our mother's favorite.

She was an odd duck who let us raise ourselves.
For Christmas we got things she'd found
in the street.

We cry ourselves to sleep like we used to.
In the morning, the milk is gone.

II

The Sun Is Worried

The sun can remember when it was a mere billion
years old. It recalls telling itself, *Plenty of time*.

Now it seems like it won't be long till it turns
into a red giant which will burn into a white

dwarf. These changes are bad news for Earth,
the sun's favorite planet. So full of life:

plants swapping carbon dioxide for oxygen,
people flocking to the beach where they

swim and listen to "Sunshine Reggae"
on their iPods. Yet all of that is in jeopardy now.

Thinking about the future upsets the sun.
That provokes mysterious spots and solar flares

which baffle scientists, keeping them glued
to giant telescopes. The sun wants to tell them,

"Stop wasting time indoors. Go on a picnic."
The sun would join them if it could, bringing

hydrogen-infused potato salad for everybody.
As it is, at the end of every day the earth turns

its face away. Grown-ups think of dinner and gin
as children wave from the back of the minivan,

"Good night, sun. See you tomorrow."

Listen, I'm Serious

You can't unkiss what has been kissed.
No matter what the body part:
lips or throat or tattooed wrist.

Kisses aren't like words easily dismissed.
They tend to go straight toward the heart.
You can't unkiss what has been kissed.

You can't unwait a waiting list.
You can't unpaint a painter's art
that features lips or throat or tattooed wrist.

You two roamed the hot metropolis
never dodging Cupid's dart.
You can't unkiss what has been kissed.

You said it was a kind of bliss
disquietingly damp and mildly tart—
those lips and throat and tattooed wrist.

You kissed them without prejudice.
You vowed to never be apart
dear lips, dear throat, dear tattooed wrist.

You can't, you can't unkiss what has been kissed.

Red Redux

She and her grandmother are content inside
the wolf. It's dark and very warm.

Plenty of time to chat. Red learns how difficult
her mother was as a girl. Learns how Grandma
had a sister who died young.

Inside a wolf is the perfect place for secrets.

They hold each other tight when they hear
the axe in the door and the woodsman's
tantrums.

Here comes the part they hate—wolf
in pieces, woodsman enormous, teeth bared,
bloody axe in his fists, his eyes undressing
both of them at top speed.

Silk

You wear a dangerous nightgown
like the women

in movies I adore: swanky
white telephones,

.38s in the end table beside
the bed.

I'd be a terrible gangster.
I can't stand being

away from you, so no
shootouts and car chases.

Somebody else would have
to handle the snitches,

finks, blabbermouths
and double-crossers,

while I ran a bubble bath
and found something

on the radio that you
could sing along with.

I don't think wise guys
would understand until

I showed them a picture
of you in that nightgown.

How it picks up the light,
slips off one shoulder.

Where I Live Now

it never snows and rarely rains but my TV points at
the blizzard in Missouri where a hundred people wait
out the storm in a high school gymnasium.

The camera pans across cots arranged beneath an idle
scoreboard. It hovers over a sleeping child, then rests
on women setting out paper plates on a table as long
as a runway.

I imagine the TV crew finally putting away their equipment
and sitting down with the others. They aren't from New York
or even St. Louis, just an affiliate some fifty miles away.

But they're trapped, too. Out there animals are perishing
and probably a bachelor farmer too stubborn to leave
his cattle.

Maybe the PA wanders around in her beautiful,
impractical shoes. Maybe she talks to a pretty 4H girl
who might want to go to college.

She carries a plate piled high with carbs and finds a seat
beside two men arguing about nitrogen content and manure.
Anybody her father didn't agree with was a cabbage head,

which is what he called her as she left for Kansas City
and her mother stood behind the screen door
of the mud porch with a cat in her arms.

"Notes, Letters and Billet-Doux
Will Soon be a Thing of the Past."

—*Newsweek*

What a shame. St. Paul wrote letters.
Pamela is all letters. There are notes
everywhere in Shakespeare, usually
carried by a loyal nurse.

Sure, there are e-mails and texts
but those are never tied with ribbon
and hidden in a secret drawer

so that someone going through
his dead wife's things lets the pages
fall to the carpet as he marvels
at the person he thought he knew.

Double Vision

In high school, the most popular girls
were the Johnson twins. Jane and Joan.
I was attracted to Jane and left a note
in her locker.

Joan met me after social studies. She said
Jane liked me, too, yet her eyes, Joan's,
were flirty and provocative.

Joan told me to meet Jane after school.
When we were alone, Jane whispered,
"Kiss me with a lot of tongue
and call me Joan."

At the Spring Fling as Jane and I danced,
Joan cut in. Then Jane returned and she
and Joan danced together.

I got dizzy and had to be driven home
by Jane, though it could have been Joan
in an identical lavender formal.

I was always on edge. Whose hand was I
holding? Whose voice on the telephone?
Who wanted to borrow my math homework?
Who was flirting with my friend Rick?

I was sixteen. I thought love was something
on a record, music pouring out of the dashboard.

The night we broke up, Jane was joined
by her sister. As I pulled away from that house
for the last time, one was crying and one
was waving. But which one?

Last night

at a taco joint a couple go at each other while their four-year
old moves a tiny brontosaurus around the table.

He dips its head into the hot sauce and the guacamole.
It stands in the refried beans.

Suddenly a tyrannosaurus looms from behind the chips,
"Why do you have to dress like such a slut."

The boy's mother plucks the dinosaur from the beans
and wipes its feet on her napkin. She pushes her son's hair
back so she can kiss his forehead.

He takes his mother's hand, opens it up and makes a bed
for the monsters to lie down in.

I Like to Kiss

up against a chain link fence. White pickets too
churchy, wrought iron too Victorian. I like to be
outside an abandoned car lot, the weeds pushing

through the concrete and the fence wrecked just
enough to give a little as the kiss takes over
and delirium sets in.

We're still on our feet and although that might
change I don't care. I could stand there half
the night holding on,

my fingers curled in the diamond-shaped spaces.
I'm breathing as hard as any punk in any movie
running from the cops

who scrambles up and over a chain link fence
except I'm not going anywhere. I'm here drunk
on these pitiless

kisses as I claw at the fence like the animal I
for the moment am.

from *The Secret Diaries of Mary Wollstonecraft Shelley*

Christmas eve 1817. I wonder about my father.
How big a fool have I been? I rarely feel well
and Percy is relentless. There are bats every night.

I am twenty years old and not unattractive.
An infant, the prospect of which frightened us both,
is buried in England. Percy sports about

with Claire Clairmont. Her name sticks in my throat.
Thomas Jefferson Hogg is attentive and relieves
my depression a little. His name disgusts me. I forgive

Percy. I do not want to be with me, either.
Byron limps about spouting poetry. The rain
is unrelenting. Everybody smells. Ghost stories

at night and in the morning Lake Geneva smooth
as a child's forehead. Tonight Percy wants a sonnet
competition. Claire claps her hands like a ninny

in a book about ninnies. Horace Smith will compete
with Shelley. A gnat meets an eagle. A damp match
and a bolt of lightning. I am ordered to bring

paper and quills and plenty of wine. I am wary
of telling Percy my dream. He's a poacher and a thief.
I fetch and carry. I bend low enough for the Hogg

to see more of my breasts. There in the fire
is a scene from my novel: terrified peasants
brandishing torches, a castle in flames.

"Can You Tell Us a Little About Your Wife?"

She stops at Scenic Viewpoints and photographs the other side of the road.
She's followed by household pets, some of them complete strangers.
She wanted a pitchfork for her fiftieth birthday.
She courts adversity with powerful cocktails.
She uses chapped lips as an excuse for everything.
She once served alphabet soup that spelled out *I am yours and yours alone.*
She tends to leave the car running like a getaway driver.
She likes being sized up by any passing meter maid.
She reads sonnets, then asks, "Hast thou moweth the lawn?"
She wept in Mexico seeing a donkey painted to look like a zebra.
She weeps every time she helps her ailing mother with her makeup.

All the News

I'm blowing on my coffee as energetically as the Big Bad Wolf when he huffed and puffed on those houses of straw and sticks, so I'm not surprised when BBW slips into my kitchen, takes the chair beside mine, and says, "Once those pigs built that sturdy brick house they thought they'd put something over on me. But what I do now is howl all night. I watch the lights go on and off as the swine careen from room to room in a panic. Two have turned on the third. They sent me a note saying that if someone should happen to be locked outdoors at noon on a day to be arranged would that be enough to make the howling stop?" When I look dubious, the wolf shows me the terrible contract which resembles in its treachery and deceit the front page of my newspaper lying right beside the butter and jam.

III

"The Only Violin in Eden"

—Robin Ekiss

Because it isn't shaped like an animal, Eve
doesn't know what to make of it.

Adam says, "We should probably ask God."
Eve frowns, "Oh, what does He know that we don't?"
Adam laughs, "Probably everything, honey."

Eve likes being called *honey*. All God ever does
is drop by while she's making a nice vegan lunch
and ask, "What have you two been up to now?"

Evening comes. Adam dozes off. Eve picks up
the violin.

A serpent lounging nearby says, "God has one
that He plays for the angels, but you could
play for Adam."

When Eve simply plucks the strings, everything
looks up from grazing. Even the redder than red
tulip leans toward her.

"Oh, play some more," the serpent says.
"You sound just like Him. Only better."

Orpheus Hearts Eurydice

He wrote that on a wall just outside
the entrance to the underworld.

It was the first thing he wanted her to see
when he brought her back to life.

We all know how that turned out.

Every day he passes the radiant scrawl
on his way to work, and it kills him.

He remembers their nights at the roller
rink—her ankles in those red, high-top

skates. Making out afterwards, his lyre
better than any radio.

Reception to Follow

When we visit the home place, I play with the chickens.
First I collect eggs for Grandma. Then I hypnotize my favorite
Rhode Island Red.

I whisper that now she's able to drive the Buick.
Then we take off together. I wave to farmers
who stare googly-eyed from their tractors.

When we get back, my father orders the chicken out,
then inspects the Buick for scratches and dents.
"How did this happen?" he asks.

That's what I remember this afternoon standing here
in the black suit: the look of astonishment on my father's
handsome face.

Waiting for the Library to Open

A man in a black hat stands off to one side. Ill at ease,
he makes enough smoke to calm bees.

Someone scolds her phone, "If you don't love me,
why did you talk about how things might be?"

Cars speed past celebrating love on the rocks.
A young woman defiantly pulls up her faded socks.

When the enormous door finally swings open,
we enter cautiously, like people at the ocean.

Inside, I sit beside a plaster bust of Walt Whitman
who celebrated all sorts of men and women

but especially Peter Doyle who drove a streetcar
and sported an extremely attractive scar.

Some days Walt would bring dandelion wine
and accompany Peter to the end of the line,

every atom of him thinking of the evening ahead—
bathwater running, the blue suit crumpled on the bed.

My Grandma Took the Train to Minneapolis

So her house, all by itself at the end of a rutted lane,
seemed perfect.

I told my girlfriend I had to look at the livestock
first. Shirley helped me into my grandmother's rubber
boots, and kissed me good-bye like she meant it.

When I hurried back, she was at the kitchen table.
Her sweater and skirt folded neatly beside her
math book.

"We can't," I told her. "I think one of the horses
is dead."

We walked out to the south pasture.

There they were—the one called Grey Prince
on his side, Chester standing. If I even felt for the latch,
all I saw was huge, yellow teeth.

My girlfriend walked right in and tugged at Chester's
mane. The horse sighed if horses can sigh.

Me in my grandmother's boots. Shirley in her practical
underwear and Chester's star-marked forehead pressed
against hers.

Tonight

I'm watching *Crime of Passion* with Barbara Stanwyck.
She's Kathy Ferguson, a popular columnist who falls for

honest cop Bill Doyle. He's easy-going and likes things
the way they are. But she says, "Oh, Bill. I want you

to amount to something." Everybody watching this movie
anywhere in the world tonight knows what follows ambition

like that: murder. What a comforting thought. Not the one
about murder, but the one about other people watching with me.

Even if they laugh and kiss as the movie rolls on without them,
when Kathy steals that gun everyone brings their eyes back

to the screen just as I do. She confronts top cop Raymond Burr
who sneers and says, "Forget it. Bill's not the man for the job.

I know what I said the other night. It was just pillow talk."
That's when Kathy takes the gun out of her cashmere coat.

The next morning. Bill drives her to the station. The camera
lingers at the entrance to the precinct. The corridor is as long

as the one she'll take to the gas chamber. I turn the TV off.
I find the blue mug you gave me and drink from the Brita pitcher.

In the sky-world, the unborn begin their narratives.
In the underworld, Charon carries souls across the Styx.

Men at Work

For driving way faster than anybody else,
I do hours of community service along
the 10 freeway. I get an orange coverall
and somebody else's gloves. There
must be a hundred Big Gulp cups.

I'm paired up with a guy named Justin
who says the debris along the 101
is primo. Once he found some pants that
fit his cousin. Then he looks down

and there's a wallet. No license or plastic,
no cash but in the little sleeves where
anybody else might keep snaps of his wife
or kids there's nothing but holy cards.

Jesus and his mom, of course. And then
some real doozies: the Novena of the Infant
Jesus of Prague and Our Lady Undoer
of Knots.

I drink some lukewarm water.
I hear rats rustle through the ivy.
"Hope this dude's alright," Justin says.

I tell him about the priest who made me
memorize patron saints: Bernadette for
shepherds, Florian for chimney sweeps,
Valentine for beekeepers.

A saint for anyone who did anything.
There's probably even one for Justin and me:
guys by the side of the road doing penance.

Sodom

She watches Lot lose one job after another
and never take the blame. At home,
he threatens to backhand her, then lies
on the floor and plays with the dog,

his hands in the dense fur, the long snout
and the drool.

She's got her kids and a few friends, women
she meets at the marketplace. She makes them
laugh: "What's that dog got that I don't?"

Then they trade bride-dresses. Putting them
on, pretending things turned out different.

That they met earlier or were widows.
That they could all live together somewhere
with trees and grass.

So when angels come there it's just for some
home cooking. Maybe help with the dishes
or tell the little kids a story.

Relaxing mostly before they have to move
on to one city or another with the often
disturbing news.

Yahweh Barbie

Forget Nurse Barbie with her pink stethoscope. No more
Firefighter Barbie who checks her makeup before rushing
to the blaze.

Yahweh Barbie is jealous and angry. She is a devouring
Barbie. Imagine her at Becky's next tea party with pretend
this and pretend that and a kitten in a bonnet.

Barbie will bring a whirling tempest. Oreos and Ritz crackers
utterly destroyed. Becky's frilly room a wasteland.

DreamHorse running amok. DreamCamper exploding
with Ken inside.

The army of Bratz will bend the knee and avert every eye
since, "Thou shalt have no other dolls before Barbie."

They Came, Took the Books Away, and Left New Guidelines for School Visits

"This is where Fiction used to be, stories that people
made up. Over there is History, reports of fruitless
opposition that are best forgotten.

"Way back there is where the DVDs were, mostly
films directed by renegades and agitators.
In that corner newspapers competed for headlines
that upset everybody unnecessarily.

"Poetry was by the tall windows. Slim volumes
so dusty and harmless they could have stayed
but they were swept up with Historical Fiction
and its twin falsehoods.

"Fantasy was disruptive, Romance pornographic,
Music a meaningless activity. But Sports stream
24/7 on all our devices. Remember to tune in
and cheer. It's required.

"Let's pause right here at autobiography which
means people telling their own stories—
'This happened to me but it wasn't my fault
and I didn't know it was wrong and I'm sorry.'

"So here we are at the main desk. Thanks for
coming. I see a few of you want to linger
in the stacks where your favorite author
used to live.

"I understand, but lingering is forbidden.
Curfew is very soon. We have just enough time
to remind you that we are open weekdays
until 7:00 p.m. and weekends until 5:00."

The Cat Who Doesn't Like Anybody
But My Wife Lolls in Ezra Pound's Lap

In the fifties, pianists named Ferrante and Teicher
sat at twin pianos. My mother and her sisters

swooned as twenty fingers ran up and down
the keyboard and they

pictured the falling leaves that stand for time
passing, for aging and death.

I find "Autumn Leaves" on YouTube and play it.
Sure enough. It all comes back—the ash trays,
the coffee cups, the tears.

Ezra strokes his beard, then the cat. "That had
nothing to do with death, Stupid. Those ladies
were wondering

what it would be like to have twenty sensitive fingers
running up and down their heavy, neglected bodies.

"That's why I keep saying 'Make it new!' But you
like to muck around in the past.

"By the way, I love this cat. I'm taking him with me
when I go."

A Crash Test Dummy Tells All

Before us, auto manufacturers used animals, especially pigs. Data was collected from the anesthetized creatures, but they were essentially sacrificed. The general public recoiled in horror at the sight of a pig at the wheel of a Ford Fairlane. Many viewers grew up with Porky Pig. They asked, "Hasn't Porky suffered enough? A fat-shaming nickname, debilitating stutter, and now this? And what about Petunia? What's she supposed to do on her own? My next car will be a Toyota!" Outrage made us inevitable. We don't mind the crashes. We have as many as 200 sensors all over our bodies. We can be used again and again. Nevertheless, all films are kept in-house and under lock-and-key. Recently as a test car careened toward the barrier, #370 shouted at #249 about a MasterCard bill. Detroit doesn't want that going viral. No matter how realistic. No matter how many lives might be saved.

Pal the Pony

Pal was always small and shaggy. Romeo the racehorse
was big and sleek. He reared and pranced and talked trash.
Pal spent most of his time moping in the barn. Finally he
trotted into town and right to the general store. "What can
I do for you today?" asked Clem. Pal used his hoof to point to
a large bottle of poison marked with a skull and crossbones.
"You know, my friend," said Clem. "I'm no big city psychiatrist
with a degree from a leading medical school and thousands
of hours of internship, but I know a little about jealousy
and vengeance. I wear an apron and sell bacon and beans.
Don't you think I want to gun down every silver-spurred
gunslinger in a fitted black shirt? You're a fine-looking pony
with a golden mane. I hate to think about prison with cretins
and degenerates just waiting for you to take a shower. So here's
my plan. Come and work for me. We can make deliveries
in a charming little cart. While I, shall we say, banter with
the lonely housewives, their pesky brats can feed you carrots
and tell you what a pretty little thing you are." Sure enough.
While Clem was busy indoors, Pal gave the kids rides. They
petted him all over and watched him drink cool well water
from a battered pan. Trotting home one evening, Romeo
passed them all lathered up, eyeballs bulging. The rancher's
ne'er-do-well son whipped him left-handed and hissed
through clenched teeth, "I bet the farm on you, numb nuts.
Win the big race or else!"

The Dixie Diner

Some friends of Elvis, Tommy and Mae, bring him
a song they just wrote called "Heartbreak Hotel."

Tommy admits he got the idea from a suicide note.
It just said, "I walk a lonely street."

That story knocks Elvis for a loop. Colonel Tom
Parker thinks the song is morbid, but Elvis records
it, anyway, even though it haunts him.

When he can't sleep, he gets in his pink Caddy
and just drives. And guess what happens—
"Heartbreak Hotel" comes on the radio.

He doesn't like to think about the bellhop who can't
stop crying, the grim desk clerk offering a key
with an unlucky room number.

He pulls into a diner, leaves that sneer in the car.
An old couple sits over coffee. He's reading
the newspaper and every time his wife tries to say

anything he snarls at her. Now the song seems
trivial, mere entertainment, something Elvis can
shake his hips to. This is lonely street—

blabbermouth cook, tired waitress, narrow aisle
from the cash register to the booth, exhausted
meringue on the last slice of yesterday's pie.

IV

The Bride of Frankenstein

no no no no no no no no no no no no no no no no no no no no no no no
no no no no no no no no no no no no no no no no no no no no no no no
no no no no no no no no no no no no no no no no no no no no no no no
no no no no no no no no no no no no no no no no no no no no no no no
no no no no no no no no no no no no no no no no no no no no no no no
no no no no no no no no no no no no no no no no no no no no no no no
no no no no no no no no no no no no no no no no no no no no no no no
no no no no no no no no no no no no no no no no no no no no no no no
no no no no no no no no no no no no no no no no no no no no no no no
no no no no no no no no no no no no no no no no no no no no no no no
no no no no no no no no no no no no no no no no no no no no no no no
no no no no no no no no no no no no no no no no no no no no no no no
no no no no no no no no no no no no no no no no no no no no no no no
no no no no no no no no no no no no no no no no no no no no no no no
no no no no no no no no no no no no no no no no no no no no no no no
no no no no no no no no no no no no no no no no no no no no no no no
no no no no no no no no no no no no no no no no no no no no no no no
no no no no no no no no no no no no no no no no no no no no no no no
no no no no no no no no no no no no no no no no no no no no no no no
no no no no no no no no no no no no no no no no no no no no no no no
no no no no no no no no no no no no no no no no no no no no no no no
no no no no no no no no no no no no no no no no no no no no no no no
no no no no no no no no no no no no no no no no no no no no no no no
no no no no no no no no no no no no no no no no no no no no no no no
no no no no no no no no no no no no no no no no no no no no no no no
no no no no no no no no no no no no no no no no no no no no no no no
no no no no no no no no no no no no no no no no no no no no no no no
no no no no no no no no no no no no no no no no no no no no no no no
no no no no no no no no no no no no no no no no no no no no no no no
no no no no no no no no no no no no no no no no no no no no no no no
no no no no no no no no no no no no no no no no no no no no no no no
no no no no no no no no no no no no no no no no no no no no no no no

Piece Work from the Garment Factory

We'd been playing ball with some kids from Webster
and that turned into a fight.

Stopping by Scotty's house for Cokes seemed like
a good idea. Then there they were—all these brassieres
draped across

the sewing machine and the couch: big brassieres
and little brassieres, sturdy brassieres and dainty
brassieres.

We dared each other to put them on. Scotty found his
mother's cigarettes. We held those and empty highball
glasses.

We prowled around in our brassieres smoking
and drinking, saying things we'd heard our mothers say:

My feet are killing me. There's not enough hours
in the day. What's he doing out till three a.m.?

William's mother was famous for crying, so he cried.
We gathered around him in our droopy brassieres.

"They're all bastards," we said. "Selfish bastards.
We'd be better off without them."

It was just another game that didn't end in a brawl.
"Let's get out of here," somebody said.

So we helped each other with the snaps and straps
and hooks and eyes. We returned the cigarettes
to the pack. We even washed the glasses our lips
had never touched.

Aphrodite to Ares

You don't even bother to wash the stink off before you
drop by fresh from a slaughter.

War, war, war. It's all you think about. I'm another
enemy, aren't I. Something else to impale.

Yesterday I left Olympus in disguise and wandered
a marketplace. Someone fell from a second story and died.

I made a kind of circle with the others. His wife threw
herself across the body.

In these clothes I resemble a mortal. What if I could die
like one, sprawled on a similar street?

The legs that held you like parentheses, the neck that Homer
described as round and sweet.

Would you even push the cur away that came to lap
my blood? Or would you stand there

one hand on the hilt of your sword wondering who
was around to drink with and gamble.

The Getaway Race

A single handicapper has the grandstand almost to himself now. Bartenders
count tips. A waitress slips off one shoe and flirts with her best customer.

The book of the day turns toward the last short chapter. The alphabet of animals
is just a few letters away from Zebra.

For some, it's time to get away, skip the last one, beat the traffic.
Toss the tickets on the table: nobody's going anywhere on that train.

Eleven fillies file into the walking ring to end the day.
Advice falls onto the jockeys' shoulders like the first snow in Eden.

Sun lights up fragrant peaks of the San Gabriel Mountains.
At the Turf Club gate, rich people wait for someone to bring the swan boat around.

"The uneasy trance will never break."

—A. Alvarez

There I lay with a piece of apple caught in my throat.
I wasn't dead. I wasn't alive, not in the usual sense.
Trance is the perfect word. Uneasy trance.

I could see the same sky move from light to dark, to light
again and again and again.

Always a dwarf to stand guard. They took turns like they
took turns cooking and washing up.

Sometimes Happy polished the glass coffin. Bashful
looked askance. Alone with me, they bared their souls.
They didn't know I could hear.

I can't repeat the things they said. They're private beyond
privacy, a privacy transmuted into mystery.

They loved me truly. One kiss from any of them and I
would have sat up and yawned. Maybe they didn't want to
stand on a box. Maybe they didn't know how to kiss.

I was bored as any figure in a snow globe. I was happy to see
the Prince. He loved me in the customary true love way.
After his customary kiss, I got to take a deep breath.

As I said good-bye to the dwarves I whispered to each
of them, "Your secret's safe with me." They wept like
children and held onto my skirt as I tore myself away.

Stopping by Woods on a Snowy Evening

Wally drives the snowplow. He's the one who told me,
so I get in the Land Rover and take a look.

Everybody knows who owns that land. My father and his
father before him. And now me.

Sure enough, there they are. Tracks from an old-fashioned
sleigh. And horse shit.

So he stayed awhile. In the middle of the night
in the middle of a snowstorm.

I take this kind of thing personally. That's my land,
my trees, my snow.

There's no secrets in this village. Some kiss-ass
snitch will stop me after church with a name.

The timber alone is worth a fortune. If somebody's laying
traps for my foxes, he'll be one sorry son of a bitch.

"the husband has a husband, the wife has a wife"

—*Li Zhiyong*

Wouldn't that be nice. Not another couple, but another mate.
They're different, not clones. Fair vs. dark, maybe. Thin
vs. substantial. Or with slight differences, but real ones.

But the husband belongs to the husband, the wife to the wife.
There's no crossing over. No swapping. This isn't 1972 again.

One night, they're all watching a scary movie together.
Something comes out of the fog. The bowl of popcorn tips over.
Nobody bothers. They're completely engrossed, glad that none
of them is really in danger.

Afterwards they stretch and yawn. What if the husband's husband
had a husband and the wife's wife a wife. Then there would be
somebody to pick up the popcorn.

King Kong Talks about His Childhood

Skull Island was the only home I knew. The natives worshipped us.
Mom would hold me up and they would bow down.

When she died I tore up a dozen acres of jungle. I buried her myself,
and that was tough. *Now what*?

I guess I wondered what was beyond the fog that always shrouded
Skull Island, but I wasn't about to swim out and look around.

I remember Mom sitting down with me every afternoon, teaching
me words like *shrouded* and asking me to use descriptive language

in my essays. Before she'd send me out to play she'd say,
"These lessons might not serve you on this island, sweet pea,

but maybe on another. There's always room for a well-rounded
individual in any society."

After she passed and I was at my loneliest I'd find my corrected
homework with her comments:

Good! Showing real improvement. Hard work does pay off, honey.
Watch for S-V agreement.

I'd read every word out loud, frightening the natives who probably
thought I was praying but, since I was a god, to whom?

It's After Dinner

Everybody's glued to CNN, so I pour some more wine
and wander away.

Two kids under a small table. Each one with a toy
car. They're making them crash into each other.

One says, "All the whores in your car die."
The other counters, "All the vampires in your car die."
"Vampires can fly away." "Whores can fly, too."

"Can't." "Can." "Can't." "Can." That goes on and on.
Finally they look at me. "Can whores fly?"

"It depends," I say. "Call girls, probably, get to fly
sometimes. Regular working girls, probably not."

That seems to settle things. Then more accidents:
Off a bridge into a river. CIA drones. Giant meteors.

One says, "All the passengers in the bus commit suicide."
The other, "Okay, but how?"

That seems to stump them. They roll their cars
thoughtfully. They look at me again.

I say, "How about if everybody eats spiders until their
brains leak out of their ears."

They make room for me under the table.

Rapunzel at Eleven

She lowers her hair for the prince, then
braces her feet against the wall to help
him climb. He's just a kid like her.
All they do is kiss, but there's hours
of it. He can tell by the angle of the sun
when it's time to leave before his
mother starts to worry. Today he
mumbles, "Uh, I don't know how to
say this but your mom died. Your
real mom." Rapunzel says. "For sure?"
The prince nods, "Dad told me. The king,
I mean." Rapunzel thinks for a moment.
"Okay, thank you." Alone, Rapunzel waits
for the witch. She'll bring dinner, then
empty the chamber pot. Would her real
mom do that? She gave her away like
a leftover. No, the witch is her mother.
She raised her, fed her, brought her books.
Told her about boys, what awful thoughts
they have. Yet, the prince isn't like that.
He's kind and thoughtful. He likes to do
what she likes to do. Her situation, though
peculiar, is not that bad. She has a mother
and a boyfriend. Both of them care for her,
just in different ways.

I Spake as a Child

I was just a kid when another kid said he didn't believe in god. He believed in his dad who was big and had a beard when nobody had a beard except the TV cook on a TV cattle drive. His dad also dispensed justice and mercy and threw real dollar bills around. He had a wife named Mary, which made everything sweeter. So we prayed to him, and he said, "My darlings, my darlings, what mischief have you been up to?" Then he picked us up one by one and kissed us loudly on our faces, something other gods never did. But then one day poof! Our god was gone. Overnight and stories started. But isn't that the way with gods? They appear in a pillar of El Roi-Tan smoke, they testify, they dispense love and hope and perform some miraculous thing or two like getting somebody a bike used but so what because let's face it everything as they say is 'shrouded in mystery.' The patrons of Ray's Tap Room say they saw him ascend. Others say he never really left. Some claimed he told them he had to go but made big plans to come back so we started counting on that even though some ordinary fathers saw the U-Haul and heard him screaming at Mary and his kids to get their asses in gear, a funny way for a god to talk but he was always different from other gods so we still loved him and prayed without ceasing.

The Creature

wanders away from the castle. People stare.
It's probably his outfit, that too-short jacket
and pants.

He goes window-shopping in the village. Admires
an Italian wool suit with a tailored silhouette.

He steps inside. The salesman stammers that
he doesn't have anything in his size and suggests
A Really Big & Tall Shop a few blocks away.

That night the salesman can't eat a bite.
He tells his wife how terrible he feels about
the way things turned out,

thugs galloping past his shop with torches,
a classic lynch mob.

He had something in the back room that might
have fit the creature. Why didn't he lead him
to the three-way mirror?

Take a tuck here and there to accentuate
the broad shoulders, get on his knees with pins
in his mouth and make the cuffs break just right.

Household Gods

Lares are spirits of the dead who protect the home.
Panes are gods of the kitchen and pantry.

Thanks to the *panes* there are no weevils in the flour,
olive oil still green, peppery and bright.   Would those things
have happened anyway? Maybe.

But the salt isn't where I put it last, the curry powder
has moved to the brink of the second shelf.

As for the *lares*, pictures of my parents and grandparents
fill a shadowbox above my desk.

Every morning I look at the photos—my father holding
an ice cream cone. My grandmother with a hatchet.

Here is where the mystery deepens: some mornings one
person or another is missing from the photo.

Grandfather revisiting his death when a tractor tipped over.
My mother on another errand in the spirit world.

My Friends and I Wanted to be Movie Stars

Big and strong, blonde and sexy. Rich and famous with new,
made-up names.

Hollywood was a way out of the Midwest. We saved allowance
money. We mowed lawns.

We'd travel like hobos, only cleaner. Sneaking out of the boxcar
at Union Station or at the sight of the first orange.

We'd sleep outside under a special moon. Fruit would fall on us
like a bunch of Isaac Newtons.

That sounded so great maybe we'd just stay and not be stars.
Costars, maybe. Or daredevil stuntmen.

But we'd be there. Where things happened. Nothing happened
in the Midwest except everybody died every night.

Maybe we'd be like Hollywood pets. Pampered, stroked, fed
by hand, loved in ways completely foreign to us.

Message from Another Planet

It's not bad here. Dusty, but we knew that and brought
highly technological masks that look like us. So that
working under the moon (everything is slightly upside down)
we know exactly who our companions are.

Love here isn't earth-love. Early on we decided against
marriage so we practice instead a kind of wide-ranging
fondness, which along with the hard manual labor
may account for our deep and restful sleep.

Now that I think about it, earth-love wasn't exactly love
either, was it? Your last transmission mentioned
"other arms and lips."

That's the kind of thing that made me sign up for
the rocket.

The Natural World

We're sprawled on the wide library lawn
with some plump dogs.

One seems to be reading over his owner's
shoulder but is just dozing.

The wind tiptoes in, but it's been so still
we all look up when the trees move a little.

Above us, pigeons loop and veer. They could be
scraps of a love letter

some lesser god has torn up and thrown
at the sun.

Things and How They Work

1

In grade school a girl who could draw
guided my hand while I tried for a horse
that resembled a horse.

I didn't mind that she was better at drawing.
I could play shortstop and she couldn't.

I told my parents about her. They said, "Well,
maybe she could draw blueprints."

They were practical. Art was just short
for Arthur. From school right to work.
Like the thigh bone connected to some
other bone.

Everybody worked. All the time. My math
teacher, Mr. Taylor, put on a white apron,
a paper hat and handed ice cream cones
across a counter all summer.

My hometown wasn't much, but one part
of it was a real Christmas card: Miller's pond
froze over every winter and we could skate there.
With a fire and everything.

Mr. Taylor showed up with his littlest daughter.
He was a really good skater. *Graceful.*
Not a word I'd say out loud then, but he was.

My mother was there, just waiting for me
and watching. When I sat down for a minute

she said, "He's been to Rome. Isn't that
something?"

How did he end up in a small town east
of the Mississippi, a town that worshipped
high school basketball and especially
our skyscraper center who could score outside
the paint, too?

I didn't actually ask but my mom whispered,
"Things don't always work out, honey."

I started to ride my bike by Mr. Taylor's house.
What things didn't work out for him, the skater
from Rome?

Sometimes he waved, sometimes not, probably
lost in thought. I liked taking phrases like that
apart:

Thought as a place someone could get lost
in, like a national park, but with no bears.
Not real ones, anyway.

Once I saw his wife standing in a blow-up kiddy
pool smoking a cigarette and crying, holding
her house dress up around her knees.

And then I'd think *house dress house dress
house dress* until it turned into somebody
whispering in another language.

2

Basketball was a language everybody understood.
Jack, Marcus, and I listened to away games on
the radio and went to home games.

We liked being at the high school where we'd
end up. The halls were wide and didn't smell
like disinfectant so much.

There were trophy cases. Famous graduates.
Some not so famous who we could see every
day behind a counter or fixing a car.

Friday nights, the gym was a madhouse.
Jack's mom went to Mass every day and twice
on Sunday, so he called the gym

Shrine of the Deadly Hook Shot because Terry
Armstrong besides being six-ten was unstoppable
with his left hand.

The town was like a graveyard during home games.
Even the cops and the firemen were there, hoping
nobody called in, then taking it easy on the parties
afterward.

"Going to state," everybody said. "Terry'll win
it for us. It's his last year!"

Then the team went to Oak Park for the regionals.
They looked big even on the radio. They outscored

us and outran us. Their center blocked shot after
shot. We lost 102–68. And that was that.

Things don't always work out.

The old guys who drank coffee every morning
at Gus's dug a grave and pushed Terry into it.
They called him a traitor and a coward and a
fuck-up.

He finished the year, graduated and got a job
selling Oldsmobiles.

My friends and I rode by the car lot, saw him
standing around in a suit that belonged to a giant.

Then Simic Motors put up a rim behind
the service bays and a customer could go
one-on-one with the star salesman.

We watched Terry in hard-soled shoes
handle fat guys at lunchtime, hitting from
anywhere until one day he got into it
under the basket and broke some guy's nose
with an elbow. A guy who did not drive off
the lot in a new Rocket 88.

After that, the backstop came down.
Terry kind of melted into the town
like everybody else who lived there
and probably planned to die there.

He married Marsha Noyse from Troy.
They went to St. Louis for their honeymoon.

Jack, Marcus and I got together every night.
We roamed the town on our bikes, knew back
streets and alleys.

Terry's house was our last stop because he shot
one hundred free throws after dinner. One miss before
he got to one hundred and he'd start over.

Almost dark, the sound the ball made
dropping through the net so fast was like
people whispering in church.

If he saw us over there he didn't let on,
or maybe he liked spectators—three where
there used to be hundreds.

Once the ball bounced off the rim and,
glowing like a planet, rolled out of the driveway
and toward us,

"Little help," he said finally. One of us tossed
it to him. Marsha came out of the back door
holding a baby. She watched him start over.

"What the fuck, Terry." We looked at each other,
me and Marcus and Jack I mean, and grinned.

We said "What the fuck, Terry," all the time
for awhile. We'd stare at a giant cone from
Dairy Delight and say it.

A girl we knew would look at us and smile
so we'd say it. Jack would make a circus
catch in left field and we'd say it.

Terry stopped shooting free throws.
When we cruised by, we heard the baby crying
and them arguing. So we didn't want to say
it anymore.

Then one night there he was again. Marsha
on the back steps with the kid on her lap,
counting for Terry, waving the baby's arms
at one, two, twenty-two, forty-five.

We counted, too. Not loud but we did it.
"Don't miss," Jack whispered. Seventy-five,
eighty-three.

A wind pushed the trees around.
Their shadows came for us, then stepped
back. We held our breath at ninety-nine.

Swish.

Marsha stood up. Held out the baby, and Terry
took it.

"See you guys," he said without looking at us.
The door closed behind them. The porch
light went out.

Biographical Note

Ron Koertge, a longtime resident of South Pasadena, taught at Pasadena City College for thirty-seven years. A prolific writer, he has published more than thirty books of poetry and prose. Some of his most recent books are *Fever* (Red Hen Press 2006), *Indigo* (Red Hen Press 2009), *The Ogre's Wife* (Red Hen Press 2013), and *Vampire Planet* (Red Hen Press 2015). He is the recipient of grants from the NEA and the California Arts Council and has poems in two volumes of *Best American Poetry* (1999 and 2005). A recent Pushcart Prize winner, he is also the author of "Negative Space," the prose poem upon which the stop-motion film by the same name was based and was shortlisted for an Oscar in Animated Short Films in 2018.